£1-00

Greatest
MOMENTS OF
CRICKET

This edition first published in the UK in 2008
By Green Umbrella Publishing

© Green Umbrella Publishing 2009

www.gupublishing.co.uk

Publishers: Jules Gammond and Vanessa Gardner

Printed and bound in Poland

ISBN: 978-1-906229-76-4

Greatest
MOMENTS OF
CRICKET

by RALPH DELLOR and STEPHEN LAMB

CONTENTS

CONTENTS

THE BIRTH OF THE ASHES

England v Australia, The Oval 1882

Despite the taut nerves amongst those watching, or not daring to watch, the cricket at the Oval on September 12th 2005, there were no confirmed reports of medical emergencies or gnawed-off pieces of umbrella handle. Another critical difference between that day and August 29th 1882 at the same ground was the outcome. Little more than 123 years earlier it was Australia who won, and so the Ashes were born.

There were other significant contrasts. The 1882 game, played on a capricious, rain-affected pitch, lasted a mere two days. The participating legends were not Warne and McGrath, but Grace and Spofforth. The latter, Australia's first great fast bowler, was the key influence on the course of one of Test cricket's classics. After taking seven wickets in England's first innings to keep the tourists in touch, he repeated the feat in the second to bring off a sensational victory.

For Australia, the one-off Test began most unpromisingly. They were bowled out for 63 by the Yorkshireman Ted Peate, who made good use of helpful conditions by opening the bowling with his left-arm spin, and Dick Barlow's miserly left-arm slow-medium. But by the end of day one England had been dismissed for just 38 runs more than Australia had managed. Frederick Spofforth bowled unchanged from the start of the innings, yorking WG Grace for just four and sending down 36 and a half overs to finish with seven for 46.

Overnight rain and a heavy downpour on the second morning made for near-impossible conditions for England, who were unable to open with Peate because the ball was too slippery. Australia's Hugh Massie made the most of the opportunity, with a half century at almost a run a ball, including nine boundaries, ensuring that the arrears were wiped off in half an hour. Although wickets fell as the conditions improved, England's grip on the game had slipped, much as their bowlers had done in the wet footholds at the outset.

Massie was fortunate on two occasions, a missed run-out and a dropped catch by Bunny Lucas at long on off Billy Barnes that incurred the audible wrath of the crowd. He eventually fell for 55 with Australia still only 28 runs in front, but the captain Billy Murdoch marshalled the middle order

In Affectionate Remembrance

OF

GLISH CRICKET,

HICH DIED AT THE OVAL

ON

th AUGUST, 1882,

lamented by a large circle of sorrowing friends and acquaintances.

———

R.I.P.

———

The body will be cremated and the ashes taken to Australia.

and tail as wickets tumbled regularly. One of them – that of Sammy Jones – fell controversially as Grace broke the wicket with the batsman out of his ground, believing the ball dead after completing a single. Murdoch was ninth out for 29, after another shower had forced the players to take an early lunch. Australia were eventually dismissed for 122, leaving England a victory target of just 85.

Their captain, Albert Hornby, promoted himself to open with Grace, but for the fourth time in four Test innings he was no match for Spofforth, now breathing fire at England that might have been fuelled by the great Oval gasholder behind him. "This thing can be done!" the Demon had insisted to his team-mates between innings, and now his words were borne out with wickets. Hornby lost his off stump for nine with 70 still needed, but after Barlow fell first ball, a partnership between Grace, batting masterfully given the conditions, and George Ulyett took England to 51 before Ulyett played inside a searing delivery from Spofforth.

It was not Spofforth but Harry Boyle who struck next, altering the tempo of the innings. With England needing just 32 for victory, Grace, on precisely that score, mistimed a drive to Alec Bannerman at mid-off. 53 for four. Twelve successive maidens followed from Boyle and Spofforth, and as England froze in the tension it is not hard to imagine one spectator dropping dead, or another, reportedly a man of the cloth, nervously gnawing at the most famous umbrella handle in cricket history.

Although Alfred Lyttleton eventually managed a single, four more maidens followed and England were choking. One batsman was said to have entered the arena with his throat so hard that he could hardly speak. The last five wickets gleaned just seven runs as Spofforth, scenting the kill, took four for two in his last seven overs. In the aftermath of victory he was carried shoulder-high to the pavilion by his team.

The trauma engendered by England's defeat – they fell seven runs short of their target – had unique repercussions. Shortly after the match the famous mock obituary appeared in the Sporting Times, lamenting the death of English cricket, the cremated remains of which were to be taken to Australia. Although no ashes were placed in the famous urn for another five years, by which time Ivo Bligh's England were extracting revenge Down Under, that lugubrious publication provided the oldest rivalry in international cricket with its now permanent title.

BRADMAN FAILS!

England v Australia, The Oval 1948

Hollies pitches the ball up slowly and ...he's bowled. Bradman bowled Hollies nought. What do you say under these circumstances? I wonder if you see the ball very clearly in your last Test in England, on a ground where you've played some of the biggest cricket in your life and where the opposing side has just stood round you and given you three cheers and the crowd has clapped you all the way to the wicket. "I wonder if you see the ball at all."

The words of John Arlott commentating on BBC Radio are recognised as a classic passage of broadcasting. He was capturing the moment when Don Bradman played his final Test innings. He walked to the wicket needing just four runs to ensure that his career would finish with a Test average in excess of 100. As it was, he had to settle for a mere 99.94. The next highest average of those playing 20 matches or more in well over a hundred years of Test cricket stands at 61.

Bradman was a phenomenon. Throughout a first-class career that extended from 1927 to 1949, he averaged a century every three visits to the wicket. His first-class average was 95.14, his top score was 452 not out – a record at the time – while his highest Test innings of 334 against England at Headingley in 1930 also established a new benchmark.

With statistics like these, it is easy to overlook the quality of the play while marvelling at the magnitude of the achievement. Bradman did not necessarily bat in an eye-catching style for he neither blasted the ball with great power, nor did he lash it to all parts in the air. In 80 Test innings he hit only six sixes, preferring to play the ball along the ground, relying on timing and placement. Spectators and fielders alike would be unaware that he was scoring quickly, yet soon after he had arrived in the middle a quick glance at the scoreboard would reveal that he had 30 to his name already.

Bradman was once tested to see if his eyesight was better than anyone else's; it was not. He merely had an outstanding ability to judge flight, and with the most

BRADMAN FAILS!

nimble footwork ensured that he maintained balance to execute his chosen stroke. It is often said that the great players do the simple things better than others. Bradman applied that simple formula for success more diligently than anyone before or since, which was why his dismissal at the Oval in 1948 sent shock waves throughout the cricketing world.

The only other time he gave a hint of mortality during his most illustrious of careers was during the 1932/33 Bodyline series. By concentrating on bowling short to a leg side field, Douglas Jardine's England managed to restrict him to 56.57 in that series. Had he maintained even that figure throughout his career he would still have featured high in the list of career averages.

As it was, he went to the Oval in 1948 with an average of 101.39. With England bowled out for 52 and Australia already having reached 117 when the first wicket fell, it was always likely that it would be his last innings. He was given a standing ovation all the way to the middle. Leg-spinner Eric Hollies was the bowler; Bradman played the first ball, but the second, celebrated delivery from the Warwickshire spinner was a googly that Bradman would normally have played in his sleep. However, on this occasion he overbalanced, the ball got past his defensive push and he was bowled.

Bradman himself did not dwell on the emotional side of the event, rather playing down the significance. "I'm very sorry that I made a duck, and I would have been glad if I had only made those four runs so I could finish with an average of 100. It was very emotional, because I knew that it might be the last time that I'd bat in a Test match. Norman Yardley, a very good friend of mine who was captain of England at the time, called all the players around me and they sang, "For He's a Jolly Good Fellow" and gave me three cheers. Some people said I got out because I had tears in my eyes, but that's rubbish."

The moment lives on, but it scarcely made a difference in the wider world of cricket. Arthur Morris scored 196 and Australia won by an innings and 149 runs to secure the series four-nil. Bradman did not bat in a Test again and it is ironic that such a great man should be remembered as often for an innings in which he failed, as for all those that were triumphs.

THE ASHES REGAINED IN CORONATION YEAR

England v Australia, The Oval 1953

Lindsay Hassett's Australians had plenty to live up to when they arrived in England in April 1953. On the previous tour, Don Bradman's "Invincibles" not only retained the Ashes but were also the first team to win four Tests in England. The hosts had last regained the urn amid much ill feeling in Australia under Douglas Jardine in 1932/33, only to surrender it in the ensuing series, at home 18 months later.

In fact it had taken England 15 Tests to beat Australia after the Second World War, one more than they had needed after the First. The breakthrough had come in 1951 when Freddie Brown's team, 4-0 down, won at Melbourne thanks largely to the efforts of their indefatigable seam bowler Alec Bedser, who finished the rubber with 30 wickets. To emphasise Australia's strength at that time, it was their first defeat in 26 Tests.

By 1953 England were led by Len Hutton, and Bedser's bowling was the primary reason why England managed to reach the final Test at the Oval with the series level. He took seven wickets in each innings in the first Test at Trent Bridge, a game England would probably have won but for rain on the last two days.

At Lord's a great match was saved by a legendary stand. After hundreds from both captains and Keith Miller, and eight more wickets for Bedser, the final day began with England needing 322 and Australia requiring seven wickets. With the hosts wobbling on 73 for four, the left-handed Willie Watson was joined by the stalwart Essex all-rounder Trevor Bailey, who kept him company for over four and a half hours. The pair put on 163 amid much tension, with Watson making 109 and Bailey 71 to deny Australia.

Rain was again the winner at Old Trafford, and at Headingley Australia controlled proceedings from the moment Hassett put England in and Hutton

was bowled, second ball, by Ray Lindwall for a duck. Despite more heroics from Bedser, who took six for 95, the tourists took a first-innings lead of 99. Their eventual target was 177 at a rate of around 5.25 an over, and positive batting from Arthur Morris and Neil Harvey left them needing 66 in the last 45 minutes with seven wickets left.

Hutton, to Australia's chagrin, decided to play for the draw. While Bedser shut down one end, Bailey held to a defensive line outside the leg stump at the other, conceding just nine runs in six overs. Whether he has yet been forgiven by his opponents for taking seven minutes to bowl one of them is a moot point, but for the second time in the rubber, and in his alternative discipline, he ensured that England retained parity in readiness for a climactic encounter that would hold the nation's attention like no other in recent memory.

Hassett's apparent good fortune in winning his fifth consecutive toss was rendered a chimera by humid conditions at the Oval. England had picked Fred Trueman for the first time that summer and it was an inspired choice, complementing Bedser's accuracy with genuine firepower. They shared seven wickets and Australia had Lindwall (62) to thank for lifting them from 160 for seven to 275. Yet again Bailey balked Australia; after Hutton made 82 he contributed a dour 64 to ensure a slender lead.

Jim Laker, brought on as early as the sixth over, started Australia's second-innings rot, trapping their captain lbw for 10. He and his Surrey team-mate Tony Lock then worked their way steadily through the order; despite an exhilarating half century partnership for the seventh wicket between Ron Archer and Alan Davidson, Australia were dismissed for 162. Lock had taken five for 45 and Laker four for 75 and England needed just 132 to bring the Ashes home.

Thanks to Australia's never-say-die bowlers, it took them three and a half hours. The great Lindwall, who finished the rubber with 26 wickets, bowled an 11-over opening spell, and neither he, nor Miller nor Bill Johnston – who bowled unchanged for 23 overs - was easy to get away. Hutton was run out with the score on just 24, but Peter May stayed with Bill Edrich to etch out 64 priceless runs. Edrich was then joined by his "Middlesex twin" Denis Compton who, shortly after three o'clock on August 19th, swung Morris to the boundary at backward square leg.

England's eight-wicket victory sent the crowd of 15,000 into unbridled euphoria. "What a scene here!" enthused commentator Brian Johnston as the ground was flooded with supporters who massed in front of the pavilion to salute their heroes. Staging the last Test of the summer as it habitually does, the Oval has provided the backcloth to many historic moments of which this, surely, was one of cricket's greatest.

MAY AND COWDREY UNRAVEL RAMADHIN

England v West Indies, Edgbaston 1957

The first England innings of the Edgbaston Test in 1957 went very well for 'mystery' spinner Sonny Ramadhin. He bowled 31 overs to take seven for 49. From another 98 overs, opening the bowling in the second innings, he finished with figures of two for 179 after Peter May and Colin Cowdrey put on a record partnership for the fourth wicket. It is fair to say that after the little Trinidadian had bowled a record 129 overs in the match, the English batsmen had worked him out.

The West Indians had arrived in England with a growing reputation as cricketers on the international stage. They were understandably naïve in their early days of Test cricket. However, they recorded their first victory in only their sixth match, and won a series at the fifth attempt, against England in 1934/35. In those days, England deemed it unnecessary to send their first team to the Caribbean, but the loss then, and again in 1947/48 and at home in 1950, spurred them into taking the West Indies more seriously. Events justified that policy when the full side under Len Hutton drew the series in 1953/54.

The 1957 West Indians were unbeaten in their first eight first-class matches. Their performance in the respective first innings of the Edgbaston Test confirmed their all-round strength. England won the toss, batted, and were bowled out for 186 as Ramadhin spun his magic. He could bowl his standard off-break and the occasional leg-break with what appeared to be the same action to the hapless batsmen, seven of whom fell to his guile. In fact, it required 56 from the last two wickets to enable England to reach that meagre total.

The West Indian reply was substantial. A superb innings of 161 from Collie Smith was supported by major contributions from Clyde Walcott, Frank Worrell and Garry Sobers, taking the West Indies to 474, a lead of 288. England faced a

MAY AND COWDREY UNRAVEL RAMADHIN

massive challenge to make their opponents bat a second time, let alone save the game, even though the pitch was looking decidedly more benign than during their first innings.

England's number three was Doug Insole, and in later years he recalled in after-dinner speeches how, on his way to the ground, he was told that the pitch was now so good that: "England will reach a million in the second innings. Mathematicians will realise that there are six noughts in a million, and I promptly got one of them!" Insole's departure – bowled Ramadhin – left England on 65 for two, and early on the fourth day Brian Close was out to make the score 113 for three.

It was at that point that Colin Cowdrey walked out to the middle to join his captain, Peter May. For much of the innings Ramadhin was bowling in tandem with Denis Atkinson, whose medium-paced off-cutters were accurate if not particularly threatening. At least not when the English pair took advantage of what was then the lbw law, permitting batsmen to pad balls away outside the off-stump without offering a shot. It was turgid stuff, not in any way attractive to watch but thoroughly effective in blunting the attack.

By the end of the day they had taken the score on to 378 for three, representing a lead of 90. May had played the definitive captain's innings with 193 not out, while Cowdrey was on 78. But they had not finished yet. They continued on the final day until Cowdrey was out for 154, an innings that had endured for some eight hours and 20 minutes. The pair had added 411 for the fourth wicket, at the time the third highest partnership in all Test cricket and still the record for the fourth wicket and for any wicket for England.

May remained unbeaten on his highest Test score of 285, made in 10 hours, when he declared on 583 for four, setting the West Indies 296 to win in 60 overs. So dispirited were the visitors after fielding for 258 overs that they were hanging on desperately at the finish on 72 for seven, with captain John Goddard still not off the mark after 40 minutes at the crease.

May and Cowdrey had seized, or perhaps assumed, the initiative for the hosts with their laborious efforts. England won convincingly at Lord's, Headingley and the Oval to take the series three-nil, but the implications of the fourth wicket partnership at Edgbaston were not confined to the result. The practice of kicking away balls outside the off-stump became so prevalent that the law was changed, enabling the bowler to win an lbw decision if the batsman is not playing a shot. So the game evolves.

AUSTRALIA AND WEST INDIES IN FIRST TIED TEST

Australia v West Indies, Brisbane 1960

The West Indian side that toured Australia in 1960/61 did not start auspiciously. Of their six warm-up matches only the fixture against Victoria was won, and that was followed immediately by an innings and 119-run defeat by New South Wales. Nevertheless, after the sensational first Test in Brisbane and what followed in the rest of the tour, the West Indians were seen off from Melbourne with a ticker-tape parade through the streets, cheered by an estimated crowd of half a million. Frank Worrell's team had captured the public imagination like no other.

Before 1960 there had been only three meetings between the two countries, all won comfortably by Australia. What made the difference this time was that the West Indies were captained by Worrell. He had the diplomatic skills to weld the players from the diverse islands of the Caribbean into a unified team, and gave the individuals contained in it the freedom to express their immense natural talent. Furthermore he was opposed by Richie Benaud, who unflinchingly accepted Worrell's challenge to play cricket in an exciting, adventurous manner hitherto largely unseen in the Test arena.

Worrell batted first on winning the toss in Brisbane, despite a brittle line-up. The decision appeared to have backfired when the score stood at 65 for three, with Alan Davidson bowling superbly. But another left-handed all-rounder rose to the occasion. In an innings of less than three hours, Garry Sobers scored 132 with 21 fours to rescue the tourists, along with contributions of 65 from both Worrell and Joe Solomon, 60 from Gerry Alexander and even a 50 from Wes Hall at number 10. The West Indies totalled 453, the runs coming from 100.6 eight-ball overs.

The basis for Australia's reply of 505, scored at an almost equally frenetic rate, was an epic innings of 181 from Norman O'Neill, while Bobby Simpson fell just eight short of a century. The West Indies batted throughout the fourth day to reach 259 for nine, before being bowled out on the final morning for

AUSTRALIA AND WEST INDIES IN FIRST TIED TEST

284, leaving Australia a target of 233 in a little over five hours to win. Playing for a draw did not appear an option, even when Hall, bowling with undiminished zest, reduced the hosts to 92 for six. That was when Davidson was joined by Benaud.

This pair hauled Australia from the depths, with a stand of 134 that left them needing a mere 27 runs for victory with half an hour and four wickets in hand. The new ball was taken, but it was a direct hit from Solomon at mid-wicket that ran out Davidson to end the crucial partnership. Wally Grout took a single off his first ball so that when Hall began the final, climactic over, six runs were needed for Australia to win whereas the West Indies needed three wickets. The odds were on a home victory.

Grout took a leg bye from the first ball, before Benaud tried to win the match off the next and was caught behind. Five to win, two wickets to fall. Ian Meckiff defended the third ball before the batsmen scampered a bye to the wicket-keeper, and Hall missed the chance to run out Meckiff when the ball was thrown to him at the bowler's end. Hall then dropped a high catch as Grout went for a big hit, allowing the batsmen to go through for another run. The next ball was despatched towards the boundary by Meckiff but cut off by Conrad Hunte, whose return to the 'keeper was good enough to run Grout out as he tried to complete a match-winning third run.

The scores were level as last man Lindsay Kline came in to face the last two balls. He played the first of them towards square leg; Meckiff was backing up well, but Solomon struck again, hitting the one stump at which he had to aim and, amid frenzied scenes of joy and dismay, the 498th Test match became the first to end in a tie. The next, and, to date, only other tie in Test cricket, came in the 1,052nd match in 1986 between India and Australia in Madras.

After an exchange of wins in the second and third matches, the Adelaide Test was drawn, but not before Rohan Kanhai recorded a hundred in each innings, Lance Gibbs took a hat-trick, and Ken Mackay and Kline held out for nearly two hours in a last-wicket partnership to save Australia. Some 90,000 people saw the first day of the deciding Test in Melbourne, which remained tense through to the final day when Australia won by a mere two wickets. Everyone present was perhaps a little surprised that it too did not end as a tie.

COWDREY THWARTS WINDIES DESPITE BROKEN ARM

England v West Indies, Lord's 1963

The light was gloomy at best, there were no sightscreens in front of the dark pavilion windows and Wes Hall, reaching speeds in excess of 90mph, had broken Colin Cowdrey's arm earlier in the innings. So it took special courage to go back out to bat with his side facing defeat. As things turned out, he did not have to face a ball on his return, but he had been prepared to do so if necessary.

One of the strongest, and most popular, West Indian sides to take the field had won the first Test at Old Trafford by 10 wickets. The Lord's contest ebbed and flowed in the very best traditions of Test cricket on a pitch that favoured the seamers. However, Frank Worrell decided to bat on winning the toss. Rohan Kanhai top-scored with 73 as the West Indies reached 301 despite fine bowling from Fred Trueman, with six for 100 from 44 overs, and 38-year-old Derek Shackleton who returned figures of three for 93 from 50.2 overs in his first Test for 11 years.

England replied with 297, thanks largely to a magnificent innings from Ted Dexter, who mastered difficult conditions and a vibrant attack to crack 70 from 73 balls. At the other end Ken Barrington was his obdurate self, taking over three hours for 80. Fred Titmus, the off-spinner not required to bowl in the West Indian first innings, contributed a valuable 52 not out, confining the tourists' lead to a mere boundary.

The West Indies were in all sorts of trouble in the second innings at 104 for five. Basil Butcher and Worrell, however, wrested back the initiative so that at the end of the third day it was the visitors who appeared to be in the stronger position. Butcher was unbeaten on 129, Worrell 33 not out with the score on 214 for five. However, in a 25-minute period on Monday

COWDREY THWARTS WINDIES DESPITE BROKEN ARM   27

COWDREY THWARTS WINDIES DESPITE BROKEN ARM

morning, those last five wickets went down for 15 runs in six overs. Butcher was ninth out for 133, but the morning belonged to Trueman and Shackleton who finished with five and four wickets respectively. England had plenty of time to score the 234 set for victory.

With John Edrich, Mickey Stewart and Dexter all back in the pavilion with only 31 on the board, there was also ample opportunity for the West Indies to force victory. Barrington again stood firm, as did Cowdrey until, on 19 with the score at 72 for three, he received a brute of a ball from Hall that broke his left arm just above the wrist. Brian Close joined Barrington in the middle, but the light was poor and after two stoppages, play was called off at 4.45; England 116 for three (effectively four with Cowdrey's arm in plaster) and another 118 needed.

The final morning was spoilt by drizzle and bad light. A resumption was not possible until 2.20, with the pitch still making life difficult for the batsmen facing a refreshed Hall and Charlie Griffith. Only 18 runs came in the first hour, during which England lost Barrington for 60. Jim Parks battled well with Close, and Titmus again took up the challenge so that England reached tea on 171 for five, still needing 63 to win in 85 minutes. With the weather always a consideration and the West Indies averaging 14 overs an hour, that equation became slightly less straightforward.

When Titmus and Trueman were out to consecutive balls after tea with the score on 203, Close changed his strategy. After playing with the utmost caution, he went on the offensive. He thought nothing of going down the wicket to Hall and Griffith, and if his body was battered, so too were the bowlers. Close was eighth out for a thrilling 70 with the score on 219. Shackleton joined David Allen with 15 runs needed, nine minutes remaining and any one of four results still possible.

So they still were when the last over, from Hall, started with eight runs needed. Singles were taken off the second and third balls, but Shackleton was then run out trying to give the strike to the more proficient Allen. Cowdrey came to the middle with two balls remaining, but he was not on strike. Allen blocked both and the match ended in the most exciting draw imaginable. Enlivened by the result at Lord's, England won at Edgbaston, only to lose at Headingley and the Oval to end the series with a three-one deficit. Despite all the other matches ending in positive results, the highlight of the entire rubber was undoubtedly the epic encounter at Lord's.

ENGLAND REGAIN THE ASHES IN AUSTRALIA

Australia v England, Sydney 1971

In the long history of Anglo-Australian rivalry, two bald measurements reflect the achievement of Ray Illingworth's side in 1970/71. He was the first captain since Douglas Jardine, in 1932/33, to win the Ashes back Down Under, and the feat has not been emulated since. So it is the one occasion in 73 years – and counting – that the deed has been done. It also ended Australia's 12-year custody of the urn, which they had regained under Richie Benaud in 1958/59.

Ahead of the tour Illingworth considered England's chances to be very good, after they did rather better against a star-studded Rest of the World team in 1970 than the 1-4 scoreline suggested. Bill Lawry's Australia, meanwhile, had been trounced 4-0 in South Africa a year earlier. England's aim was to win through pace. It mattered not that their spearhead finished unimpressively in the 1970 domestic averages; John Snow was born to play Test cricket, and the sight of a baggy green cap at the crease provided him with a more rousing motivation than day-in, day-out county cricket.

If Snow was the key bowler in 1970/71, Geoff Boycott was the most influential batsman. After Snow, who was to take 31 wickets in the series, had begun with a six for 114 in the drawn first Test at Brisbane, Boycott produced solid innings of 70 and 50 in the second at Perth, which also ended without result. The third at Melbourne was completely washed out, leading to the rapid organisation of the first one-day international. To Illingworth's irritation, an extra Test was also scheduled in at the MCG for later in the tour. Meanwhile at Sydney England went one up, largely through Boycott (77 and 142) and Snow at his quickest, who tore through the hosts in their second innings with seven for 40.

Draws followed at Melbourne and Adelaide, after which Australia, for the first time in 70 years, dropped their captain. Lawry was replaced for the final Test back at the SCG by Ian Chappell, and England, without Boycott, whose arm had been broken by Graham McKenzie in a one-day match just four days earlier, were put in on a bowler-friendly surface. They made just 184, but picked up two quick wickets late on to set up the most dramatic day of the rubber. With Australia closing in despite the loss of seven wickets, Terry Jenner, more spin bowler than batsman, ducked into a short ball from Snow and was hit on the head.

With the crowd erupting after Jenner had been helped off, bringing back memories of 1932/33, Snow was cautioned by umpire Lou Rowan for short-pitched bowling. After a drinks interval in which cans were thrown on to the outfield, Snow went down to field at long leg, where he was briefly grabbed by a drunken spectator. With bottles now being thrown as well as cans, Illingworth led his team off, refusing to return until the ground was cleared and his team's safety assured. Play eventually resumed after a delay of just seven minutes.

Australia took their innings into day three, building a lead of 80, and England's second-innings total of 302 left the hosts needing 223 to win, their only chance of retaining the Ashes. Again the drama revolved around Snow who, after yorking Ken Eastwood in his first over, dislocated a finger attempting a catch, a mishap that ended his involvement in the match. After Peter Lever accounted for Ian Chappell, Illingworth decided to bowl himself, ushering in his finest hour as England's captain. At 71 Ian Redpath was held at short leg, and at 82 Doug Walters rose to the young Bob Willis' bait, slashing a wide one to deep gully, placed for the purpose. After Keith Stackpole fell trying to sweep Illingworth, Australia were 123 for five at stumps.

The key batsman at the start of the final day, with 100 needed, was the captain's hugely talented younger brother. Greg Chappell advanced down the wicket and missed Illingworth's out-floater for Alan Knott – whose brilliance behind the stumps had bolstered England throughout – to complete the stumping. Two wickets for Basil D'Oliveira followed before, shortly after 12.30 on February 17th, Keith Fletcher held Jenner at silly point off Underwood. England had won by 62 runs, taking the series 2-0 to regain the Ashes.

A brace of Johns – Edrich and Hampshire – were the two strong men who hoisted Illingworth onto their shoulders and bore the captain from the arena for the presentation. Boycott and Snow – the former with his left arm in a sling, the latter with his right – were both there to savour the ceremony. Not for the first time or the last, Illingworth had revelled in the pressure of a tight situation, guiding his young team to a triumph unique in their lifetimes.

"IF I CAN SEE IT, I'LL HIT IT"

Lancashire v Gloucestershire, Old Trafford 1971

"If we come off now, this lot will lynch us!" The Lancashire captain, Jack Bond, referred to the Old Trafford crowd in response to umpire Dickie Bird, as deepening gloom threatened to halt an enthralling Gillette Cup semi-final and extend it into an anti-climactic reserve day. Time had already been lost to rain and although the weather had cleared, it was past seven o'clock and dusk was falling. Bird had offered the light to Bond, whose team had gradually fallen behind the required rate in response to Gloucestershire's 229 for six, made in 60 overs.

Bond's offer to bat on was fatalistic. "We can't win, so we might as well continue to the end," he told Bird. The gates had been locked since that late July morning, and the famous old ground was packed to every nook and cranny, with many of the 27,000 supporters spilling onto the grass. Bond had already commented on the fading light to Bird's fellow umpire, Arthur Jepson, when he came in. In response, Jepson is reputed to have motioned to the sky and asked if Bond could see the moon, which was by then shining brightly. Bond said he could, to which Jepson replied: "Well, how much further do you want to see?"

At 8.30, it was announced that the last train to Bristol was about to leave. Such was the excitement among Gloucestershire supporters, the warning went unheeded. When Bond's partner, Jack Simmons, was bowled by John Mortimore, Lancashire still needed 27 to win from five overs – a challenging task in those days – with just three wickets left. As their young left-arm spinner David Hughes walked out to bat, it was almost quarter to nine, and the lights on Warwick Road Station were competing with the moon for brightness. "If I can see it," Hughes told his skipper, "I'll hit it."

In the circumstances he saw it remarkably well, and was as good as his word. The fateful decision by the Gloucestershire captain, Tony Brown, to persevere with Mortimore rather than revert to his quicker bowlers, ensured that one over from the off-spinner passed straight into the annals of cricketing folklore. At the start of it, there were reasonable grounds for Brown's decision; Mortimore had dismissed Clive Lloyd and Farokh Engineer, Lancashire's two most dangerous batsmen, as well as Simmons.

Hughes improvised in response to the first delivery, stepping outside leg stump to crash it to the extra cover boundary. The next, which was tossed slightly higher, was deposited over long on for six. Unaware in the hubbub of Simmons' exhortations from the Lancashire balcony to settle for singles for the rest of the over, Hughes picked up a brace of twos.

Paradoxically, the umpires' decision to end the game that day disadvantaged the fielding side more than the batting one. Once Hughes had decided on all-out attack, the chances of his holing out were always going to be slim in such gloom. Brown later pointed out that it was actually harder for the fielders at the end because they simply could not see where the ball was. The batsmen knew roughly where it was being bowled, and they had the screens to help, but the fielders had no idea and were shouting to one another if they saw the ball going in a colleague's direction.

Another four, another six, and Hughes had taken 24 off the over. The spearhead of Gloucestershire's attack, Mike Procter, returned with just one run needed for victory, and a pushed single by Bond was enough to trigger a pitch invasion the like of which can rarely have been seen at Old Trafford. Such was the excitement, the BBC had responded by delaying the 8.50 news (not the nine o'clock news, as was sometimes claimed later) until the game finished at around 8.55.

As the Lancastrian crowd surged onto the pitch, the commentator Brian Johnston said he could not remember such a sight since England won the Ashes at the Oval in 1953. The game, he said, was one of the most extraordinary cricket matches he had ever witnessed. History does not relate how or where the trainless Gloucestershire supporters spent the night; presumably it was passed partly in drowning their sorrows.

Lancashire went on to win the final at Lord's thanks to a moment of similar magnitude, Bond leaping like a salmon to take a seemingly impossible catch off Asif Iqbal, who was winning the match for Kent. It was a catch to reduce Asif to tears, which perhaps flowed in the Gloucestershire dressing room after Hughes' performance. There was no dispute when he was named man of the match – and given 24 glasses of champagne to fill – for his efforts. The victory remains one of the most famous in Lancashire's history.

WEST INDIES CONFIRMED AS ONE-DAY KINGS

Australia v West Indies, World Cup final, Lord's 1975

January 5th 1971 was the day when the first one-day international cricket match took place in Melbourne, as a gesture to ticket-holders when the first three days of the Ashes Tests were rained off. The authorities decided that as a meaningful match was unachievable in the time remaining, it would be abandoned without a ball being bowled and a 40-overs-a-side match was hastily arranged.

After 46,000 people turned up for that game, one-day matches became an established feature of the international calendar and in 1975 the World Cup of one-day cricket was inaugurated in England. To justify the event's billing as a world cup, a wider representation than the six Test countries was needed. A rather damp and squelchy qualifying tournament was held on club grounds in the Midlands, resulting in Sri Lanka and East Africa joining the major Test nations in two groups of four. South Africa were absent for political reasons.

The rain that dogged the preliminaries gave way to a hot, dry spell by the time the tournament got under way, so not a single minute was lost to the weather. The public were enthralled by the competition, and by the time the semi-finalists were known, the game was commanding attention not experienced for years.

The 'Ashes' semi was played on a Headingley ground that was at its most helpful to seam bowlers. A green, used pitch and humid, overcast conditions caused the ball to swing and seam prodigiously. Australia's Ian Chappell put England in and Gary Gilmour bowled them out.

At one time 37 for seven, England made a partial recovery to 93 all out. Australia, at 39 for six, were also struggling, but Gilmour wielded his bat as effectively as he had bowled the ball, for 28 not out from as many balls to see Australia home by four wickets. In the other semi-final at the Oval, New Zealand reached 98 for one before suffering a spectacular collapse to be all

out for 158. West Indies were 133 for one before a mini-collapse narrowed the margin of victory to five wickets.

The Lord's final was played on the longest day of the year, and needed to be, with the pulsating action lasting for all of 10 hours. Australia won the toss and fielded first, with immediate and spectacular results. Dennis Lillee induced the feisty little left-hander, Roy Fredericks, to tread on his wicket as he hooked him for six in the direction of St John's Wood Road. Gilmour and Jeff Thompson then took a wicket each to reduce West Indies to 50 for three in the 19th over.

That was when they struck back. Clive Lloyd joined Rohan Kanhai to add 149 in 26 overs. It was spectacular cricket between the imposing Lloyd and the diminutive Kanhai, causing bowlers to adjust their length just as the left-right hand combination required adjustment of line. Lloyd's hundred came from a mere 82 balls (the second 50 from 30 balls), and his side were in a strong position at the interval with 291 on the board.

Australia went after the target with a purpose. Although Rick McCosker went early, Alan Turner, Ian and Greg Chappell took the score along to 162 before Viv Richards completed his elimination of the trio with his third brilliant run out, exploiting indifferent running. Keith Boyce had taken the first wicket and claimed three more, Lloyd himself chipped in to bowl Doug Walters, and Vanburn Holder ran out Max Walker to leave Australia facing defeat on 233 for nine.

The game appeared to be up, but Australia found the unlikely batting partnership of Lillee and Thomson edging them ever closer to their target. Fifty-nine were needed when they came together, but as so often happens in a seemingly lost cause, the pair began to enjoy themselves. Cheeky runs, the odd fortuitous edge and some thundering strokes of which any authentic batsman might be proud shook any complacency from the West Indians. Some of the world's leading bowlers were being treated with near contempt by two others, who happened to be batting at the time.

However, just as the notion of an outrageous victory was taking shape, the Australian reverie came to an end. Thomson had garnered 21 from as many balls when he was the fifth run out victim in the innings, leaving Lillee undefeated on 16. They had found the boundary just three times between them while putting on 41. The West Indies won the first World Cup final by a mere 18 runs, and as Lloyd accepted the trophy and the man-of-the-match award from Prince Philip, the doubting cricket establishment had to accept that the tournament had a permanent place in the game.

BOYCOTT REACHES HUNDREDTH HUNDRED AT HOME

England v Australia, Headingley 1977

Cricket's capacity to range from the ridiculous to the sublime would rarely have been more apparent to Geoffrey Boycott than in the Ashes series of 1977. Recalled by England after three years of self-imposed exile for the third Test at Trent Bridge, practically his first significant intervention was to run out the local hero, Derek Randall. But in partnership with Alan Knott, who came in with England on 82 for five, Boycott eventually justified his selection. Both made centuries to give their team a handsome first-innings lead, which enabled them to go on and win the match.

As a result England, who had already gone one up at Old Trafford, arrived at Headingley for the fourth Test with a 2-0 lead, needing only a draw to recover the urn that they had lost under the fearsome fusillades from Dennis Lillee and Jeff Thomson in 1974/75. Boycott, with an appropriate sense of timing, had completed his 99th first-class century playing for Yorkshire at Edgbaston just a couple of days earlier. He emerged padded up from the pavilion with his captain, Mike Brearley, who had just won the toss. Brearley himself lasted just three balls before being caught behind off Thomson.

Beyond the boundary, the bookmakers put Boycott's chances of making a unique piece of history at four to one. But he could sense, from the wave of applause that greeted his first scoring stroke for two past point, the encouragement of his home crowd. Despite that, batting in the first session was not easy. Aided by the hazy atmosphere, Thomson, Len Pascoe and Max Walker all found some movement, but Boycott and Bob Woolmer saw England through to lunch on 76 for one, with Boycott needing another 66 to pass the magic milestone.

As conditions eased during the afternoon, he assumed his characteristic air of impregnability, mixing watchful defence with the clinical ability to dispatch the bad ball. The crowd's sense that their hero's wicket was key was exemplified by the muted

reaction to the fall of Woolmer in the fourth over after lunch. Randall stayed with Boycott until the score was 105, when he was lbw to a breakback from Pascoe. A critical slice of fortune followed, when all the Australians were convinced that on 75, Boycott edged a ball from Ray Bright to Rod Marsh as he tried to turn it to leg.

Bright was so angry to have the appeal rejected that he snatched his sunhat from the umpire, Bill Alley, who reprimanded him. Greg Chappell intervened to cool the situation, which promptly heated up again when Bright was no balled at the start of his next over. Tea arrived with Boycott on 79, and Thomson bowled Tony Greig for 43 shortly afterwards. After scoring just 10 runs in an hour after tea (shades of Trent Bridge, where he took two and a half hours to make his first 14), Boycott went to 96 with a single off Pascoe, giving him the strike to Greg Chappell in the next over.

Sensing the imminence of the moment, the smattering of policemen on the boundary edge took up their specified stations. On receipt of a full-length leg cutter from Chappell, Boycott leaned into it, driving it to the long-on boundary underneath the football stand. He raised both arms above his head in triumph – not a standard mode of celebration hitherto – as spectators made light of the police "cordon" to surge onto the ground. According to Bob Willis, Boycott was so immersed in the moment that he ignored the attentions of Graham Roope, the non-striker who had gone to congratulate him. Play was held up for 10 minutes and Boycott lost his cap in the melee, although it was later returned.

Although the feat of scoring 100 first-class hundreds had been achieved 17 times - John Edrich was Boycott's immediate predecessor – he was the first to manage it in a Test match. He went on to make 191, effectively snuffing out any lingering Ashes hopes in the Australian camp. Four days later, when Randall held the catch from a Marsh skier and performed a cartwheel, the man who had been so embarrassingly run out on his home ground just a fortnight earlier had the pleasure of completing the coup de grace.

"Magic!" said Boycott on the balcony afterwards, after being mobbed for the second time as he went off at stumps on day one. In all the circumstances – an Ashes Test, his home ground, and in just his second game for England after a long period in the wilderness – it was a moment that even the most accomplished magician might have struggled to conjure. "I will remember it for the rest of my life," Boycott said later. "No matter how many more noughts I make, I will remember that moment."

BOTHAM AT HIS BEST

England v Australia, Old Trafford 1981

When asked to compare Ian Botham's two great innings of the 1981 Ashes, good judges agree that the second was better than the first. So does the man himself, rating the 118 he made at Old Trafford alongside his 138 at Brisbane five years later. Both were played under pressure, both were chanceless, and both set up England wins and Ashes retention. In dramatic terms, though, there was a difference. The knock at the "Gabba" came at the start of a rubber, while the Manchester effort crowned the most compelling few weeks to be witnessed by cricket lovers in England until 2005.

The well-documented broader context when Botham arrived in the middle on August 15th 1981 bears repetition. England, struggling against Australia's attack of Dennis Lillee and Terry Alderman, had gone behind at Trent Bridge and drawn at Lord's, where Botham, his form in a trough after two unsuccessful series against the West Indies, resigned the captaincy. In the hope of restoring the successful partnership that had dominated his formative Test career, the selectors returned the job to his predecessor, Mike Brearley.

It was to be one of the most famous selections in cricket history. Brearley offered Botham the chance to miss the Headingley Test but he played, following a five-wicket haul with a half century in the first innings. However, England were forced to follow on and when Botham came in to bat a second time, they still needed 94 to make Australia bat again. His hit-and-hope, unbeaten 149 provided rumbustious entertainment, and ultimately a slim hope of victory as Australia were handed a small but unexpected target of 130.

Bob Willis' finest hour – he took eight for 43 – ensured that they fell short, sensationally, by 18 runs, making England the only team in the 20th century to win a Test after following on. A scarcely less tense denouement followed at Edgbaston, where Australia were presented with a slightly larger target, 151. The Headingley horror doubtless in the back of their minds, the tourists stumbled from 87 for three to 105 for five, at which point Botham, who had been reluctant to bowl, came on and wiped them out. He took five for 11 and England were 2-1 up.

BOTHAM AT HIS BEST

There were still two Tests to follow in the six-match series, so technically Australia could still turn things around. Shortly after lunch on that Old Trafford Saturday, they were fancying their chances. Although England led by 101 on first innings, they had poked and prodded their way to 104 for five in the second. But Botham, in at number seven, had by now become an irresistible force. Unlike at Headingley he played himself in, taking just three singles off his first 30 balls. The first signs of aggression were a cut and a cover drive, both to the boundary, against the slow left-arm spin of Ray Bright. With Botham on 28, Australia took the new ball.

At Headingley his innings had included slogs and heaves, but this time Botham's demolition job was mercilessly clinical. Two impeccable bouncers from the great Lillee were hooked for six, as though the bareheaded Botham, as Richie Benaud put it, was "smashing a fly". When Alderman dropped short, he was pulled robustly to the midwicket boundary. Given room outside the off stump, Botham smashed both bowlers past point. "When you're playing in a match, you don't necessarily watch every ball," said his team-mate, David Gower. "But when Ian Botham is in that sort of mood, then you are compelled to watch." Before an ecstatic full house, he went to his century by sweeping Bright into the pavilion.

When Botham walked off after feathering Mike Whitney to Rod Marsh after tea, he had made 118 off 102 balls, with 13 fours and six sixes, then an Ashes record. If he had given impetus to England's Ashes challenge at Headingley and Edgbaston, he had now made the bandwagon unstoppable. Alan Knott and John Emburey both added half centuries, and having hoped to chase 200, Australia were left needing 506. Although a magnificent, unbeaten 123 from Allan Border helped them past 400, the Ashes were duly retained by England when last man Whitney was held at short leg off Willis.

"It was one of the best," Botham later recalled of his innings. "That one and probably the one at Brisbane. There was the 200 against India [in 1982], and other scores, but I think that those two stand out. Both were technically good knocks, and I took the bull by the horns." Of course in 1981, critics were unable to make such comparisons; suffice to say that some of them were left asking not only whether it was Botham's best innings to date, but also whether it might have been the greatest ever played.

RICHARDS MASTERY MESMERISES ENGLAND

England v West Indies, Old Trafford 1984

Viv Richards prided himself on his ability to deliver when it mattered. This happened remarkably often at Lord's, where he excelled both for the West Indies and Somerset. But at Old Trafford on the last day of May 1984, the circumstances could hardly have been less propitious, or the need greater. After Clive Lloyd had won the toss and chosen to bat in the first of three 55-over games for the Texaco Trophy, his team were soon in trouble. The best opening partnership in the world was quickly split with the run out of Desmond Haynes by Ian Botham off his own bowling, and when Gordon Greenidge was caught behind off Botham, West Indies were 11 for two.

That was the point at which Richards joined his fellow Antiguan, Richie Richardson, and it was predictably Richards who scored the bulk of the 32 runs added before Richardson was caught and bowled by Bob Willis. On a blameless pitch, wickets continued to clatter, the next three – Larry Gomes, Lloyd and Jeff Dujon – to the off spin of Geoff Miller. When Malcolm Marshall was run out after facing just four deliveries West Indies were 102 for seven, with only the tail to keep Richards company. "Certainly we were in disarray," he said later, "with the score on that wicket, [thinking] when we bowl on it, what's going to happen?"

In such conditions England were scenting blood, although Richards now found the first of two staunch allies in another Antiguan, Eldine Baptiste, who made 26 in a partnership of 52 before being caught behind off Botham. But Joel Garner soon hit a return catch to Neil Foster, and Michael Holding joined Richards with the scoreboard showing a well below-par 166 for nine. The question from Holding: "Smokey, what are we going to do, man?" The answer: "Just keep it going, Mikey, and we'll see what happens."

An uncomplicated response, and what happened was an explosion of strokeplay that stretched the boundaries of credulity. Richards wrote afterwards: "We had no more wickets to play with and I played with great freedom. I started hitting some big sixes. Everything worked out well, and I felt totally in control." Most of his earlier runs had come on the leg side, generated by twinkling foot movement and propelled by strong forearms, supple wrists and

uncanny placement. One such stroke off Botham brought up his century, and England's attack thereafter was murdered.

Foster, trying to restrain Richards by bowling a full length outside leg stump, was dispatched inside out to the cover boundary. When he tried again, Richards took a couple of steps to leg before driving him for six over long off. An attempted bouncer was swatted to the rope at long leg, while Botham was flicked – with minimum apparent effort – into the members' pavilion on the full. The advent of Derek Pringle was promptly celebrated with two maximums, over long off and straight, the second of which took Richards past 150.

In the remaining carnage Willis was belted for six over extra cover, and the penultimate ball of the innings from Botham clipped through midwicket to raise the hundred partnership (Holding had contributed a princely 12). The only minor surprise was that Richards couldn't clear the rope from the last delivery, although he did manage to swat it to the long-off boundary. 189 not out, 170 balls, five sixes and 21 fours. England's attack, by no means the worst to take the field, shredded. Richards had already caused a one-day sensation five years earlier, with an unbeaten 153 in Melbourne to defeat Australia, but this effort outshone it. It remains arguably the finest one-day international innings ever.

As a case of snatching victory from the jaws of defeat, Richards' Old Trafford contribution must also rank high. He was not finished either, for he claimed a brace of wickets as England, their top order blown away by Garner, Holding and Marshall, fell 105 runs short of their target. Allan Lamb, whom the West Indies usually found a feisty opponent, played the only significant innings of 75 before he was last out. And all that after West Indies were 102 for seven!

As on this same ground when Botham was decimating Australia's attack three years earlier in one of the greatest Test innings, the expressions of the spectators as they stood and applauded showed that they were witnessing something extra special. Richards failed as England came back to level the series 1-1 at Edgbaston, but in the decider at Lord's – where else? – he hit them all over the park again. Eighty-four not out off just 65 balls, four sixes and 10 fours, turning a run chase into a doddle. As Jim Laker put it in the commentary box at the time: "Richards 2, England 1".

GOOCH – FROM ZERO (TWICE) TO HERO (TWICE)

England v India, Lord's 1990

Graham Gooch often remarks upon how he remembers his scores from his Test debut because they are embedded in his surname. It is a reference to the pair he got at Edgbaston in 1975 against Australia. After just one more match he was dropped, but he came back to become England's leading run-scorer in Test cricket. Having begun his career so disappointingly, it must have meant all the more to him when he set a new record at Lord's against India in 1990, becoming the only batsman to record a triple hundred and a hundred in the same match.

Gooch went into the game in form, having scored 177 for Essex in their second innings against Lancashire at Colchester. He had also reached 154 in his previous Test – against New Zealand at Edgbaston a month earlier. He averaged 101.70 in the 1990 first-class season, scoring 2,746 runs. He scored another 1,242 at an average of 69 in one-day cricket. Gooch was at the top of his game.

One can only speculate on what demons Mohammad Azharuddin envisaged in the pitch to persuade him to put England in when he won the toss. He had plenty of time to rue that decision in the field, as England progressed to 359 for two on the first day. The Indian captain had not been helped by wicket-keeper Kiran More dropping a straightforward chance when Gooch had 36. At close of play, the England opener had moved to 194 in the midst of a record partnership for England against India of 308 with Allan Lamb, who was 104 not out.

Lamb was dismissed the following day for 139, but Gooch went on in majestic form, unfurling sumptuous strokes to all quarters of the ground. He admitted to becoming a little nervous once he had got past 250, particularly during the tea interval when he was in sight of a triple hundred, but was afraid of missing out by making a silly mistake. Once he got past that mark, he cut loose.

"People asked me why I didn't go on to try to break the record," remembers Gooch. "I didn't think of it at the time. I just thought about how we would have to declare and I only kicked myself afterwards when I was out for 333 and thought I should have been a bit more

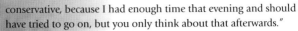

conservative, because I had enough time that evening and should have tried to go on, but you only think about that afterwards."

The record for the highest individual Test score at the time, 365 not out, belonged to Sir Garfield Sobers. Gooch was only 32 shy of that when he played a tired shot against Manoj Prabhakar to be bowled. He had been at the crease for nearly 10 and a half hours and faced 485 balls, hitting 43 of them to the boundary and three over it. It was a supreme display of batting, with record after record tumbling to the England captain. He allowed Robin Smith to reach his hundred and debutant John Morris to get to the middle before declaring on 653 for four.

India's reply showed plenty of character. Ravi Shastri opened the batting and scored a hundred. Azharuddin then played a delightful innings that showed the wristy strokeplayer at his very best. He took only 88 balls to reach his hundred, 80 of which came in boundaries. India closed the third day on 376 for six, with a draw appearing the only result. But after Azharuddin went early on Monday morning, more wickets fell so that India were 24 short of avoiding the follow-on with one wicket in hand. Off four consecutive balls from Eddie Hemmings, Kapil Dev wiped out that deficit and England had to bat again.

Gooch's response was to score another hundred. This time it was 123 to take his match aggregate to a neat 456. The runs came in two and a half hours off 113 balls with 13 fours and four sixes, in another dominant display. He declared setting India an unlikely 472 to win, but the tourists were undaunted at 57 for two overnight after less than an hour's batting. Even when Sanjay Manjrekar fell on the last morning, Azharuddin batted as if a win was not out of the question. However, wickets fell at a steady rate until Gooch ended proceedings with a throw from mid-on that ran out the last man, and England were winners by 247 runs. Gooch was declared the man of a classic match after one of the easiest decisions an adjudicator has ever had to make.

THE BALL OF THE CENTURY

England v Australia, Old Trafford 1993

"The first couple of balls you bowl are just warm-ups, and you just hope to get them somewhere near the right spot. To bowl the perfect leg-break first up – I think it was just meant to be." So said Shane Warne of the delivery that became one of the most talked about ever. Modest though his assessment may seem, it should be added that Warne was never the sort of bowler to eschew risk at the start of a new spell.

He was 23 and had been playing Test cricket for little more than a year. A solitary wicket for 228 runs in his first two Tests against India had hardly hinted at anything exceptional, and an invitation followed from Rod Marsh to return to the Australian Cricket Academy, which he had left under a cloud a couple of years earlier. Under the tutelage of Terry Jenner, Warne gave up beer and lost some weight. Recalled in Sri Lanka, he was trusted by his captain, Allan Border, to bowl in the closing stages of a tight encounter in Colombo. Warne took three for 11 in five overs as Sri Lanka fell 16 runs short. An epic journey had begun in earnest.

Such was the impression that he made on the next two series – he took seven in an innings against the West Indies and 17 in three Tests in New Zealand – Warne came into the 1993 Ashes encounter with no less a batsman than Martin Crowe canvassing him as the best leg spinner in the world. Australia were expecting their opening attack of Craig McDermott and Merv Hughes to spearhead their defence of the little urn, but they also knew of England's historic frailty against leg spin, apparent against Pakistan's Abdul Qadir a decade earlier.

Knowing Warne a little by reputation but not at first hand, England nonetheless went into the first Test reassured by the ample presence in their middle order of Mike Gatting, an acknowledged expert at playing spin. But they had to wait until day two to face Warne, because Graham Gooch gave Australia initial use of the Old Trafford pitch. It did not reap early rewards; Australia's opening pair of Mark Taylor and Michael Slater posted 128 before being parted. At stumps on day one Australia were 242 for five, and Warne opted to settle his inaugural Ashes nerves by spending the evening with Hughes, his all-or-nothing Victorian team-mate.

THE BALL OF THE CENTURY

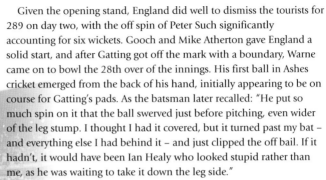

Given the opening stand, England did well to dismiss the tourists for 289 on day two, with the off spin of Peter Such significantly accounting for six wickets. Gooch and Mike Atherton gave England a solid start, and after Gatting got off the mark with a boundary, Warne came on to bowl the 28th over of the innings. His first ball in Ashes cricket emerged from the back of his hand, initially appearing to be on course for Gatting's pads. As the batsman later recalled: "He put so much spin on it that the ball swerved just before pitching, even wider of the leg stump. I thought I had it covered, but it turned past my bat – and everything else I had behind it – and just clipped the off bail. If it hadn't, it would have been Ian Healy who looked stupid rather than me, as he was waiting to take it down the leg side."

Such was his scepticism about whether such a delivery was geometrically possible, Gatting stood for a moment before confirming with the square leg umpire, Ken Palmer, that he was out. The ball had done more than just dismiss him; it had set the tone for the entire series, and indeed for more than a decade. Australia's confidence rocketed; England's was fatally undermined. Robin Smith was soon caught at slip off a barely inferior delivery from Warne, who then induced Gooch, the only England batsman to play him with any confidence, to hit a full toss to mid on. England eventually subsided to 210 all out, and lost the match by 179 runs.

Warne was to strike 34 times in the 1993 Ashes series, and England were no nearer mastering him on his final tour of England 12 years later, when he took a record 40 wickets despite Australia's defeat. Can one delivery ever have played such an influential part in the outcome of a rubber? Warne himself wrote later: "Psychologically, I think, we had struck a massive blow for the rest of the series and none of the batsmen really tried to get after me. As for being the 'ball of the century', I don't think that can be for anyone to say. So much of cricket's rich history has gone unfilmed." True enough, but no one watching was able to suggest another contender.

NEW BOYS SRI LANKA WIN THE WORLD CUP

Australia v Sri Lanka, Lahore 1996

England had been the venue for the first three World Cup tournaments. In 1987 the event was split between India and Pakistan, with another dual hosting arrangement in 1992 as matches were played in both Australia and New Zealand. In 1996, this went a stage further with a tripartite agreement featuring India, Pakistan and Sri Lanka. Of these, either India or Pakistan might have been fancied to become the first host nation to win the cup, while at least one of the hosts could reasonably have been expected to reach the final. One of the hosts did, but nobody predicted that instead of either Mohammad Azharuddin or Wasim Akram lifting the trophy, the honour would fall to a somewhat rotund 32-year-old by the name of Arjuna Ranatunga, who hailed from Sri Lanka.

India had caused a major upset in an earlier tournament by beating the then mighty West Indies in the 1983 final at Lord's, but India was an established cricketing nation and Sri Lanka were relative newcomers to the big league. The country had experience of playing one-day cricket in previous World Cups and ICC Trophy events, but it was not until 1982 that they played their first Test match. In the blink of an eye, in international cricket terms, they had gone from new boys to world champions.

Their path to the final in Lahore was strewn with obstacles, although they put such inconveniences to good use. Australia and the West Indies refused to go to Sri Lanka to play scheduled matches because of civil strife in the country, so the Sri Lankan players remained fresher than some. The boycott scarcely affected Australian or West Indian chances of progression, because three minnows had been included in the 1996 tournament. Of these, Kenya, pulled off one of the greatest upsets of all time by beating the West Indies, but were later eliminated along with Holland, the United Arab Emirates and Zimbabwe. So, the newly introduced quarter-final stage of the World Cup included all the major countries.

Sri Lanka had developed a new approach to the limited-overs game. Rather than waiting for the final 10 overs for an all-out assault, as was the accepted strategy in one-day cricket, Sanath

NEW BOYS SRI LANKA WIN THE WORLD CUP

Jayasuriya and Romesh Kaluwitharana blitzed the attack for the first 15 overs while the fielding restrictions were in force. England, to their surprise, fell foul of this strategy in the quarter-finals, while India beat Pakistan, West Indies defeated the fancied South Africans and Australia accounted for New Zealand.

Australia overcame the West Indies by five runs in one semi-final in Chandigarh, as the men from the Caribbean lost their last eight wickets for 37 runs. If that was dramatic it was nothing compared with the other semi-final in Calcutta, where Sri Lanka made 251 for eight before India collapsed to 120 for eight in 34.1 overs. It caused an explosion of unrest in the stands and the match was called off, forfeited by India.

So to the final in Lahore, the first day/night international to be held in Pakistan. Ranatunga won the toss and took the unusual step of putting Australia in. The previous five finals had been won by the side batting first, and Australia would have taken that option due to an uncharacteristic lack of attention to detail. They had only practiced during the day, whereas Sri Lanka had gone to the Gaddafi Stadium to experience the lights. It was then that they encountered the heavy dew prevalent at the time and coach Dav Whatmore, in consultation with the captain and senior lieutenants, decided to avoid being in the field as the turf, and the ball, became saturated.

By the 27th over of their innings Australia were cruising towards a substantial total, with only one wicket down and 137 on the board. That a star-studded batting line-up should then be restricted to 241 for seven says much for the perseverance of the Sri Lankans. So did the way they set about chasing the runs. The openers failed for once, but Asanka Gurusinha (65) and Aravinda de Silva, with an undefeated and perfectly paced 107, put on 125 for the third wicket. Ranatunga himself tickled the winning runs through the off side to reach 47 not out, and Sri Lanka had won a sensational victory by seven wickets with 22 balls to spare.

The rain was just beginning to fall as Ranatunga stepped forward to receive the silver trophy. As he did so, a new cricketing power emerged and as he held the spoils aloft, a war-torn country was sent into raptures of delight that continued long into that, and many another, night.

HUSSAIN 200 GIVES ENGLAND AN ASHES BOOST

England v Australia, Edgbaston 1997

Generations of insecure England batsmen, at the mercy of selectorial whims, have spoken of the need for a substantial innings early in a series to guarantee their places in the side. In 1997 Nasser Hussain would have felt unsure of his after his previous seven innings in a stop-start Test career had produced but one fifty. However, he was chosen for the first Test of the Ashes series at Edgbaston and responded, coming in with England's score standing at 16 for two, by sharing a partnership of 288 with his old friend Graham Thorpe for the fourth wicket, and going on to make 207. His place was secure for the remainder of the six-Test rubber and for the rest of his career, injuries excepted.

A product of his father's tuition, he was noted early in his time with Essex as having a special talent. He was also self-assured to the point of arrogance in one so young, and senior colleagues could not expect self-sacrifice when it came to run outs. Such an attitude did not necessarily make him a popular figure, but there was no doubting his ability with bat in hand or, indeed, as an outstanding fielder.

He made his Test debut in the Caribbean in 1990, along with Alec Stewart. However, after England's victory in Jamaica, Hussain injured his wrist playing tennis. It kept him out until the fourth Test, when normal service was resumed and England were trounced, as they were in the final Test. He disappeared from the scene until 1993, when good county form saw his return to face Australia in the third Test, with England already two down. They had the better of the draw in that match, while Hussain showed that he was ready for the highest level of the game with scores of 71 and 47 not out.

His first Test century came at Edgbaston against India in 1996, with another in the same series at Trent Bridge followed by a third in Zimbabwe the following winter. But the rich vein of form dried up and Hussain became less certain of the selectors' automatic nod.

The pitch at Edgbaston on the first morning against Australia in 1997 offered the bowlers help, and England took full advantage after Australia had decided to bat first, hoping that the surface would quickly dry out into a batsman's paradise. It did, but not before the visitors had been bowled out. Darren Gough, Devon Malcolm and Andrew Caddick were roared on by a partisan crowd who could hardly believe a scoreboard revealing Australia to be all out for 118 in 31.5 overs. It was a sensational start, but the batsmen had to make the most of the situation.

Mark Butcher, on debut, and Michael Atherton went early. Stewart did not last long, but Hussain and Thorpe then tightened England's stranglehold with their commanding partnership for the fourth wicket. Hussain began watchfully, but was beginning to blossom by the end of the first day when he was undefeated on 80. The new ball forced Hussain and Thorpe to be a little more circumspect on the second morning, but they then produced a dazzlingly complimentary display of batting. Thorpe was his usual busy self, while Hussain played with increasing freedom and authority.

After losing his partner, Hussain found another willing ally in Mark Ealham as he powered his way past his previous highest Test score, and his best in any form of cricket before reaching his double hundred. He eventually edged a leg-break from Shane Warne to wicket-keeper Ian Healy to be out for 207. In seven and a quarter hours he had faced 337 balls and hit 38 fours – many of them stroked elegantly through the covers.

It was a masterful innings, coming almost exactly 12 months after his first Test century on the same ground, and formed the basis for England to win the Test by nine wickets. The previous six Ashes rubbers had been won by the side taking the first Test, but this one went against that trend. By the time the teams left Trent Bridge after the fifth, Australia were three-one up, despite Hussain recording another century at Headingley. England won at the Oval but although Hussain played in four more Ashes series, two of them as one of England's more thoughtful and successful captains, he never captured the urn. Nevertheless, in a distinguished career, his 1997 innings at Edgbaston remains a great moment in the greatest series in cricket.

DONALD v ATHERTON

England v South Africa, Trent Bridge 1998

"Often cricket reduces itself to quite a gladiatorial aspect, one batsman against one bowler, and you tend to block out everything else, all the noise from the crowd, the noise from his team-mates, and it's just you against him, and it's a private little battle, and one to win. In cricket that's what I look forward to the most, the little individual challenges."

Those are the words of Michael Atherton, recalling his utterly compelling encounter with Allan Donald in the evening session at Trent Bridge on July 26th 1998. England, one-nil down in the rubber, needed 247 to win and so draw level with one to play. Mark Butcher had fallen early, but Atherton and Nasser Hussain were going well. Then Atherton got a ball from Donald, South Africa's premier fast bowler in his prime, which brushed his glove on the way through to wicket-keeper Mark Boucher.

"It knocked my hand off, really," Atherton said later. "Nearly broke my knuckle. I was very happy to stand there and wait for the umpire's decision and, once he said not out, carry on". The umpire, New Zealander's Steve Dunne, could hardly have known how significant his error would prove to be. And Atherton's happiness was not shared by Donald, whose mood graduated to unvarnished fury when his next delivery, a particularly rapid response, sped to the fine leg boundary off Atherton's inside edge, narrowly missing his off stump on the way.

The bowler's pace was hotting up along with his temper, and Atherton was faced with no small challenge; deliveries propelled at up to 95 miles per hour, dug in short and deliberately aimed to hit him. But he was at his best in such circumstances, even against one of the most hostile and venomous spells of fast bowling ever seen. "I was batting with Nasser," Atherton later recalled, "and we said, this is the crunch part of the game."

The working over was verbal as well as physical, and not pretty for prudish lip readers. Boucher had to launch himself skywards to take a particularly vicious delivery, which thudded into his gloves after brushing the back of Atherton's shirt. The batsman narrowly avoided another missile, possibly intended to knock his block off. Donald was

DONALD v ATHERTON

brought beyond boiling point when Boucher, a safe pair of hands thus far, dropped a straightforward nick off Hussain. There was something primeval about the consequent expression of anguished anger on the face of the bowler.

To Donald's credit, he gave South Africa's young wicket-keeper a gesture of reassurance at the end of the over, but there was no understating the implication of the moment, nor indeed of the earlier umpiring error which precipitated the drama. Atherton and Hussain required no further good fortune, although Atherton in particular was lucky not to be injured, as they saw out the fourth day with England on 108 for one, needing another 139 for victory.

Donald took the one wicket to follow on the final morning – Hussain for 58 – but South Africa's chance had gone. With Donald tiring, Atherton sensed a lifting of the shackles and accelerated, while Alec Stewart joined him to make an unbeaten 45 at a pace that was breezy even by his standards, off just 34 balls with nine boundaries. Atherton was left two short of his hundred, but had the pleasure of hitting the winning runs as England triumphed by eight wickets.

They secured the rubber in a tense fifth Test at Headingley, which England won by 23 runs with, South Africa's players might argue, the help of some more consistently erratic umpiring from Pakistan's Javed Akhtar. So that third session on day four at Trent Bridge was the turning point. How much drama would have been missed but for an uncharacteristic error by the white-coated Kiwi? "I had to try not to panic, because when the adrenalin's rushing you can lose it," Donald said later. "But I gave it everything I had for eight overs or so, and people have said it was the most electrifying spell they have seen. It was certainly the fastest that I've bowled consistently in any one spell."

Despite England's win in 1998, Donald was not slow to extract a measure of revenge. In the first over of the return series in Johannesburg late the following year, he brought Atherton forward to his second delivery, which shattered his stumps. Donald took six for 53, setting the tone for a rubber that the hosts won by the same margin. Gleeful though he must have been to get one back on his old adversary, it is that 1998 spell at Trent Bridge which will linger in the memory; raw aggression matched by gutsy resistance, of the type which Atherton relished and few other batsmen in the world could provide.

WORLD CUP TIE HAS SOUTH AFRICA IN KNOTS

Australia v South Africa, Edgbaston 1999

Most one-day internationals live in the memory about as long as an ailing mayfly. Some may be recalled simply for an outstanding innings, or a breathtaking catch. But this 1999 World Cup semi-final had pretty well everything you could wish for. If the abiding image is of Allan Donald dropping his bat after being called for a suicidal single by Lance Klusener, what about the ball from Shane Warne that dismissed Herschelle Gibbs? Such was the drama that attended the outcome, several wonderful pieces of cricket were cast into shadow by the eventual result – the first-ever tie in World Cup cricket.

It meant that South Africa, despite their customary strong start to the tournament, failed to reach the final due to an obscure regulation involving net run rate. In the absence of any announcement, this was not understood by many in the crowd at Edgbaston that day. Australia, who finished marginally higher at the end of the preceding Super Six stage of the competition, went through to trounce Pakistan in an anti-climactic final at Lord's. If spectators there felt a touch cheated, the cups – or perhaps the glasses – of those fortunate enough to be at Edgbaston were brimful with contentment.

Going into the match, Australia had drawn heart from their Super Six win over the same opposition in another thrilling encounter at Headingley. That game was memorable for the moment that allowed Steve Waugh to lead his side to victory in the final over with an unbeaten 120. Celebrating a catch before he had control of the ball, Gibbs dropped Waugh at midwicket and the batsman, on 56, reportedly – and presciently – said: "You've just dropped the World Cup." Waugh was never a player to make light of such good fortune, and he did not give South Africa a second chance.

At Edgbaston they initially had their noses in front, as Shaun Pollock took the first of his five wickets, Mark Waugh for a duck, with the fifth ball of the match. After Donald struck twice in an over to dismiss Ricky Ponting and Darren Lehmann, Australia were 68

WORLD CUP TIE HAS SOUTH AFRICA IN KNOTS

for four in 17 overs. Gritty half centuries from Steve Waugh and Michael Bevan effected repairs despite accurate bowling, particularly from Jacques Kallis, who was playing with a stomach injury and went for just 27 runs in 10 overs. A typically breezy cameo from Warne helped Australia's cause before another double Donald strike ended the innings on 213.

South Africa's reply, too, held promise until they were tripped up by the type of wizardry of which Warne was uniquely capable. After Gibbs and Gary Kirsten had taken their opening stand just two shy of 50 at around the required rate, Warne produced a perfect leg break – a replica, in fact, of his Gatting delivery at Old Trafford six years earlier – to break through Gibbs' defences. Perhaps unnerved, Kirsten was castled attempting a sweep in Warne's next over. When Hansie Cronje was taken at slip without scoring, Warne had taken three key wickets in eight balls.

Kallis and Jonty Rhodes then batted much as Steve Waugh and Bevan had to revive the South African challenge. After the pair had added 84 Rhodes fell, and Kallis, on 53, became the last of Warne's four victims. But despite some aggressive strokeplay from Pollock, they were slipping behind the rate. With 25 needed from the last 15 deliveries it was the left-handed Klusener, pummelling 31 off 14, who took them back in front and to the threshold of victory. His innings included a six and four fours, all struck with savage ferocity, and with placement to match.

By the third ball of the last over, bowled by Damien Fleming, South Africa, despite having lost nine wickets, needed just one run to win. With the fieldsmen in a ring, Klusener smashed the ball straight and Donald, the non-striker, was almost run out as he backed up too far. Losing his head, Klusener repeated the shot and charged. Donald, having grounded his bat to avoid being run out by a deflection, dropped it and set off impossibly late. Mark Waugh threw the ball from mid-on to Fleming, who rolled it to Adam Gilchrist, who broke the wicket with the horrified Donald out of his ground.

It is the nearest South Africa have come to reaching a World Cup final. Their exit from the following tournament, which they hosted in 2003, also came amid a touch of farce when they misinterpreted the Duckworth/Lewis method, thinking they had enough to win when rain ended the game at Durban, when in fact they were one short. Cricket and the bizarre tend to go hand in hand, and on both these occasions it was to the palpable agony of South Africa and their supporters.

ENGLAND TURN THE CORNER AGAINST WEST INDIES

England v West Indies, Lord's 2000

When Jimmy Adams' team came to England in the Millennium year, the West Indies were known to be an inferior force to that which had dominated world cricket for most of the previous two decades. Steve Waugh's Australians had ended the extraordinary run of 15 years without defeat, and their lethal production line of world-class fast bowlers was well nigh exhausted. Curtly Ambrose and Courtney Walsh, though still potent, were in the twilight of their careers and the batting revolved around the lonely genius of Brian Lara.

However, most pundits had doubts about whether England, dubbed the worst team in the world less than a year earlier, could win the Wisden Trophy for the first time since Ray Illingworth's side in 1969. The doubts were deepened by an all too familiar capitulation in the first Test at Edgbaston. Walsh took eight wickets, including his 450th in Tests, as the hosts were bowled out for 179 and 125, losing by an innings and 93 runs. So to Lord's, a ground with a reputation, over the previous decade, for inspiring England's opponents.

In overcast conditions Alec Stewart, leading in place of the injured Nasser Hussain, put the West Indies in, but his five-man pace attack could make no inroads in the first session. In fact the tourists reached 162 for one before losing Sherwin Campbell for 82. Darren Gough and the recalled Dominic Cork, who enjoyed playing the West Indies at Lord's, took four wickets apiece as they were restricted to 267. But England's batsmen were exposed yet again by Ambrose and Walsh. Woefully, their reply stood at nine for three, then 85 for six, before they were bowled out for 134.

Same old story, most were thinking. But not Hussain, in the camp despite his injury. According to Gough he said: "If we're going to go down this time, we're going down fighting. We're going to pepper them with aggressive, fast bowling." It was Gough who set the tone, with a great catch at third man to dismiss Campbell off Andrew Caddick. The same bowler had Wavell Hinds taken at short leg second ball, and six for two

became ten for three when Adrian Griffith was caught behind off Gough. Crucially Lara went cheaply, taken in the gully sparring at Caddick, and with West Indies on 24 for four Lord's, quite uncharacteristically, was going berserk.

Some mistake, surely? But no! Shivnarine Chanderpaul, to his visible disgust, was adjudged caught at short leg off Gough. Ridley Jacobs, flailing at a wide one from Caddick, was caught at slip – 39 for six. Without addition, after making just three from 40 deliveries, the captain was lbw to Cork, and Ambrose held at short leg (Mark Ramprakash's third catch there) fending off Caddick. Two runs later Franklin Rose pushed a return catch to Cork, who trapped Reon King lbw to end the West Indies innings on just 54.

21 wickets had fallen on a breathtaking second day, but this classic match was far from over, as England still needed 188 to win on an increasingly capricious pitch. They started badly on the Saturday, losing Ramprakash for two. But the two Michaels, Atherton and Vaughan, steadied the ship before Vaughan was caught behind off Walsh with the total on 95. The great Jamaican now revived West Indian hopes, having Graeme Hick taken at slip and, more importantly, trapping Atherton lbw for 45. England were 120 for four and it was anybody's game. Stewart played with characteristic brio before falling lbw, again to Walsh, for 18. Amid mounting tension Craig White was caught behind in the same over, and when Nick Knight fell likewise to Rose, 39 were still needed with three wickets left.

England needed a hero, and with the crowd now barely able to watch, up popped Cork. "I'll block it, you play the shots," said Gough as he joined him after the fall of Caddick. With 26 needed, Cork swung Rose into the Grandstand – the critical blow which set Lord's on fire once again. Four followed over mid on, and the pressure was eased. With just one needed a cover driven four from Cork settled the issue, and was greeted by a roar as voluminous as can ever have been heard in London NW8.

Instead of going two down with three to play, England were back on terms. It was a watershed in their rivalry with the men from the Caribbean. After Stewart managed a century in his 100th Test in the Old Trafford draw which followed, an astounding game at Headingley ended in just two days as the tourists, first unstitched by the home-grown Gough and White, were torn apart by Gough and Caddick. All England needed at the Oval was a draw, but they went one better, enabling Hussain to lift the Wisden Trophy after a 3-1 series victory.

VAUGHAN RATED BEST BATSMAN IN THE WORLD

Australia v England, Sydney 2003

It is something of an understatement to say that England have not enjoyed much success on recent tours of Australia. Since Mike Gatting's team held on to the Ashes in 1986/87, England have only won three Tests there in 26 starts. Furthermore, those wins each came in series that were decided as far as the Ashes were concerned. That was the case in 2003 when England reached the final Test in Sydney already four-nil down. Apart from three one-day international victories against Sri Lanka, they had not won a match on the entire tour. The performance of one man, however, ensured that there was something to savour from the expedition.

Michael Vaughan was 29 at the time but was playing in only his 28th Test. He had not demanded selection as a youngster, but had impressed on England A tours and bided his time in the queue for batting places. When his chance came, against South Africa in Johannesburg on the 1999/2000 tour, he suffered a traumatic debut. He went to the crease at number four with England two for two. That became two for four before he had faced a ball, and it says something for Vaughan's temperament that he survived 84 deliveries on his way to what was a creditable score of 33 in the circumstances.

It was in 2002 that he developed into a serious Test batsman, with scores of 197 and 195 against India. A failure followed in the first Test in Brisbane, but in Adelaide he alone stood between his team and ignominy with 177 in the first innings and 41 in the second. England still went two-nil down. Vaughan did not do anything conspicuous in Perth, but when the teams met in Melbourne for the fourth Test he was back to his best, scoring 145 in the second innings and almost single-handedly forcing Australia to bat again, when they suffered a modicum of discomfort chasing 107 to win.

If England needed a fillip in Sydney (and in the circumstances they needed any lift to morale they could find), they received wonderful tidings when both Glenn McGrath and Shane Warne failed fitness tests. It was the first time in 101 matches that both had been

VAUGHAN RATED BEST BATSMAN IN THE WORLD

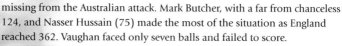

missing from the Australian attack. Mark Butcher, with a far from chanceless 124, and Nasser Hussain (75) made the most of the situation as England reached 362. Vaughan faced only seven balls and failed to score.

Australia's reply was built around Steve Waugh. In what was thought might be his last Test at his home ground (in fact he was to play two more), he managed to reach the hundred that all Australia craved off the last ball of the second day. With Adam Gilchrist thrashing 133, the hosts enjoyed a first-innings lead of one run, but would still have to bat last on a wearing pitch. It was therefore important for England to set a substantial target, and this they did thanks to another superb innings from Vaughan.

The ball seemed to be guided to the middle of his bat as he unfurled elegant cover drives and savage pulls. He shared a partnership of 189 for the third wicket with Hussain before enabling England to declare on 452 for nine. Vaughan made 183, with 27 fours and a six from the 278 balls he faced, eventually falling victim to a highly contentious lbw decision from the Zimbabwean umpire, Russell Tiffin.

England took three wickets before stumps, and wrapped it up in another 34 overs on the fifth day, Andrew Caddick taking seven for 94 in what transpired to be his final Test. England won by 225 runs to save some face, and finally to provide Vaughan with the win his batting throughout the series deserved. In the five Tests he scored 633 runs at an average of 63.3. It was not just the weight of runs that marked Vaughan out as a major success, but also the grace and authority with which he scored them. That is reflected in the fact that despite being on the losing side in four of the matches, he was named man of the series.

By the mystical equations that govern these things, Vaughan was briefly rated the number one batsman in the world, and few disputed his right to the accolade. He later succeeded Hussain as captain, and took the team forward to the ultimate goal of the celebrated Ashes victory of 2005. The magnitude of that achievement possibly dwarfed his wonderful tour of 2002/03, but perhaps the personal confidence he gained from those performances in Australia boosted the team effort that he led so tellingly two years later.

LARA LASHES ENGLAND TO REGAIN RECORD

West Indies v England, Antigua 2004

In 1994 Brian Lara set a new record for the highest individual innings in Test cricket. Against a hapless England attack on the Recreation Ground in St John's, Antigua, he played a major role in the West Indies' 3-1 series win. Amid scenes of great jubilation, he scored 375 to pass the previous record of 365 not out, set by Garry Sobers in Kingston, Jamaica, in 1958 against Pakistan. Present at the ground when Lara assumed his mantle, Sir Garfield went out to the middle to congratulate him in person.

He might not have noticed that in pulling the record-breaking runs, Lara had dislodged a bail that fortuitously fell back into the groove. It was just about the only piece of good fortune he needed in an otherwise flawless innings. That was not the case when Lara set a new first-class record just a couple of months later. Playing for Warwickshire against Durham at Edgbaston, he scored 501 not out in a match that was destined to be a draw after a day's play was lost to rain. The good luck Lara enjoyed in that innings came when he was on just 18. He was dropped by Durham wicket-keeper Chris Scott, who turned to first slip and said forlornly, "I bet he goes on to get a hundred now."

Lara lost the Test record when Matthew Hayden scored 380 for Australia against a very ordinary Zimbabwe side in Perth in October 2003. But Hayden was to hold it for only six months before Lara snatched it back again, in rather different circumstances to those of a decade earlier. Antigua was again the setting and England were again the opponents, but they were a much stronger side, while Lara was captain of the humbled West Indies.

England had won the first three Tests, and were on the verge of a whitewash to avenge the two "blackwashes" inflicted upon them by the West Indies in the 1980s. Lara was under particular pressure as so much was expected of him, yet thus far he had failed to deliver. His scores were 23 and nought in Jamaica, nought and eight in Trinidad, followed by 36 and 33 in Barbados. Exactly 100 runs at an average of 16.66 was not what his Caribbean public expected.

LARA LASHES ENGLAND TO REGAIN RECORD

He did the first thing right by winning the toss on the usual St John's batting paradise. In another manifestation of the changing order, England's pace attack had been irresistible earlier in the series, but they found the surface at the Recreation Ground to be anything but good for their health. They managed to dismiss Darren Ganga for 10 when the score was 33 in the 14th over, but that brought Lara to the crease early.

As memories of 10 years earlier came flooding back, so too did his form. The outfield was as fast as the pitch was true, enabling Chris Gayle to reach a fifty that included 10 boundaries, before he was out to the last ball before lunch. Rain then prevented any play until after four o'clock, but there was still time for Lara to put on a hundred with Ramnaresh Sarwan before stumps. Lara was undefeated on 81 out of 208 for two.

England's whitewash aspirations gave way to perspiration on the second day. Their attack toiled through 105 overs, after which the West Indies were in total command on 595 for five. Sarwan had put on 232 with Lara, but once he had gone for 90, Ricardo Powell and Ryan Hinds followed relatively cheaply. Ridley Jacobs then joined Lara to provide ideal support for his fellow left-hander.

Lara was 313 not out overnight, and although some critics accused him of selfishness when he batted on, after three consecutive defeats he wanted to make the game safe before entertaining any idea of winning it. He reached lunch with the total on 734 for five. Jacobs had his hundred, and Lara himself had gone past Hayden's 380 to dine with 390 to his name. Few now begrudged him what might have been thought of as an indulgence, in reappearing after the interval to reach 400. In all, it took him 773 minutes; he faced 582 balls and hit 43 fours and four sixes.

A deflated England made only 285 in their first innings but, following on, reached 422 for five for the match to finish in stalemate. The West Indies had their face-saving draw, while the record was back in the Caribbean, in Lara's possession once again. Of all the great names that grace that particular list of batsmen, only one appears twice: Brian Charles Lara.

"IT'S HIM OR ME"

England v Australia, The Oval 2005

When Kevin Pietersen strode to the wicket on the final morning of the utterly compelling 2005 Ashes series, England were in danger of failing, at the last gasp, to regain the urn lost 16 years earlier. The great Glenn McGrath was on a hat-trick after taking the wickets of Michael Vaughan and Ian Bell and England, at 67 for three, were still only 73 runs ahead. McGrath did eventually dismiss Pietersen – his next and final Test wicket in England – but not before the 25-year-old, in his maiden Test series, had scored 158 dazzling runs, and in doing so, secured England's triumph.

An excellent umpiring decision by Billy Bowden denied McGrath his hat-trick after the ball flew off Pietersen into the slips. Despite a vociferously confident – and unanimous – appeal, Bowden correctly ruled that the ball had come off Pietersen's shoulder. He was then missed at slip – an awkward chance to Matthew Hayden off Shane Warne via Adam Gilchrist's glove. Perhaps the costliest dropped catch of the series followed when Pietersen had reached 15, Warne himself grassing a comparatively straightforward offering at first slip off McGrath. It was to go down in history as the moment when Australia in general, and Warne in particular, dropped the Ashes.

Despite that miss, Warne snared both Marcus Trescothick and Andrew Flintoff to leave England – team and entire nation – lunching uneasily at 127 for five with 73 overs still to play. Appetites for food were scant, and mobile phones were used to an extent that the network could not consistently sustain. Such was the tension during the morning that England's chairman of selectors, David Graveney, could watch no longer and took sanctuary in his car to listen to the radio commentary. But Pietersen, despite a blow in the ribs from a ball of express pace from Brett Lee, was still there.

The gladiatorial exchange between Lee and Pietersen that followed the interval was surely one of the most dramatic passages of Test cricket seen at the Oval, or

anywhere else. Perhaps the blow in the ribs triggered it; certainly, as Pietersen said later, he decided during the break "it's him or me." Lee's next three overs went for 37 runs. Sixes abounded; Pietersen hit seven in all, an Ashes record, in an arc ranging from fine leg, through midwicket to long off.

After reaching his 50 from just 70 balls, he smashed Lee for two sixes (one of which Shaun Tait made a vain attempt to catch) and two fours. Pietersen was ably supported by Paul Collingwood for more than an hour, before the Durham man was caught at silly point off Warne. Collingwood would later be sledged by Warne for being awarded an MBE for scoring just 17 runs in the match, but his second-innings contribution was vital in the context of the game.

At that point, the all-important runs-to-overs equation was moving gradually in England's favour, but at 186 for six they were still not safe. When Tait, just after being hit for a brace of offside boundaries by Pietersen, fired a full, reverse swinging delivery into Geraint Jones's off stump, Ashley Giles appeared to play what could well rank as the innings of his life. He helped Pietersen add 109 crucial runs in a stand that finally put any possibility of victory beyond Australia. While Giles mixed defence with occasional attack, Pietersen continued to enthral the vocal crowd with his dazzling display.

McGrath ended his innings with the new ball after Pietersen had batted for four and three quarter hours. He had faced just 187 balls in making 158, including 15 fours as well as the seven sixes. By the time he was dismissed, every available rooftop surrounding the ground was populated by joyous England supporters, not to be denied their chance to witness cricketing history. Rarely, if ever, can such a critical match have been saved by an individual innings of such aggression. Although England were eventually bowled out, Warne taking 12 wickets in the match to finish with 40 in his final series in England, the draw, and consequent 2-1 series win for England, was a formality by the time the last wicket fell.

Pietersen was to score 158 again against Sri Lanka the following summer, and yet again, bizarrely, at Adelaide during the 2006/07 series in which the Ashes were so peremptorily wrenched back from England's grasp. None of the three innings featured in an England victory, but the effort at the Oval, with everything that was hanging on Pietersen's performance that sunlit September afternoon, will remain etched in the memories of all who saw it. As the celebrations began at the Oval, and extended to Trafalgar Square, Lord's and Downing Street the following day, England supporters knew that the man who had forsaken the land of the kruggerand had done them sterling service in coming of international age.

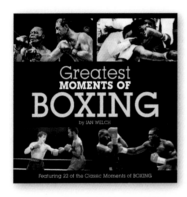

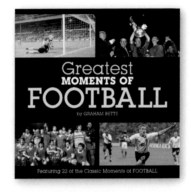

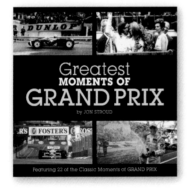

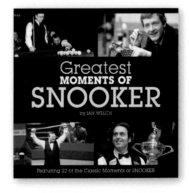

THE PICTURES IN THIS BOOK WERE PROVIDED COURTESY OF THE FOLLOWING:

GETTY IMAGES
101 Bayham Street, London NW1 0AG

Concept and Creative Direction:
VANESSA and KEVIN GARDNER

Design and Artwork: DAVID WILDISH

Image research: ELLIE CHARLESTON

PUBLISHED BY GREEN UMBRELLA PUBLISHING

Publishers:
JULES GAMMOND and VANESSA GARDNER

Written by: RALPH DELLOR and STEPHEN LAMB